Proverbs of the World

Proverbs of the World, Volume 1

Emre Imer

Published by Dives International OÜ, 2018.

PROVERBS OF THE WORLD

First edition. November 11, 2018.

Written by Emre Imer.

This book is dedicated to all the children of the world.

Introduction

What has been developing our civilization is information and it started with the drawings in caves, which humans left as their heritage, as the most important thing to survive in those days' wild life was knowing how to cope with it. As things were discovered and named, drawings turned into letters, alphabets, basically languages, and notes on the walls into books, translated and read by millions of people who lived in different centuries.

Aphorisms of wise men, such as world leaders, philosophers, authors and poets have always enlightened my own path and assisted in finding the right direction. On the other hand, the proverbs of the nameless people have been another source to getting closer to wisdom.

"Proverbs are the children of experience." is a proverb from Sierra Leone. With the curiosity to learn more about the proverbs said around the world, even in the countries I have never been to, I have decided to prepare this book to share the proverbs I liked most out of many I have found out.

"Proverbs in conversation are torches in darkness." is a Venezuelan proverb. I hope you enjoy the book and the proverbs help you in your life.

Emre Imer

Afghanistan

- A bird only flies as high as his wings take him.
- A little water is a sea to an ant.
- A river is not contaminated by having a dog drink from it.
- A wise enemy is better than a foolish friend.
- Bloom where you are planted.
- Don't be a thief and you won't fear the king.
- Don't show me the palm tree, show me the dates.
- Don't use your teeth when you can untie the knot with your fingers.
- Even the judge was drunk when the wine was free
- Grumbling and carping are the muscles of the weak.
- Hearing is never as good as seeing.
- However tall the mountain is, there's a road to the top of it.
- If a forest catches fire, both the dry and the wet will burn up.
- In the shop of the sightless jeweler, the ruby and pebble are one.
- Look after your property, and you won't accuse your neighbor of being a thief.
- One flower does not bring spring.
- One who doesn't appreciate the apple, won't appreciate the orchard.
- Patience is bitter, but it has a sweet fruit.
- The best weapon is the one that's in hand.
- The seeker is the finder.
- Unfortunates learn from their own mistakes, and the lucky

ones learn from other's mistakes.

Albania

- A day without work can yield a night without sleep.
- A tailless dog cannot express his joy.
- Don't put golden buttons on a torn coat.
- Every guest hates the others, and the host hates them all.
- Fire is a good slave, but a bad master.
- Hard heads suffer much.
- He who can read and write has four eyes.
- He who hesitates, regrets.
- If you have figs in your knapsack, everyone will want to be your friend.
- In the eyes of the mouse the cat is a lion.
- It is easy to cut the tail of a dead wolf.
- Love is sometimes difficult but death even more so.
- One eats figs whilst the other pays.
- Patience is the key to paradise.
- Sharp acids corrode their own containers.
- The fox will catch you with cunning, and the wolf with courage.
- The man who has eaten enough will never believe a hungry one
- The sun at home warms better than the sun elsewhere.
- The wolf loves the fog.
- Those who know how to praise also know how to lie.
- When a hundred men call a wise man a fool, then he becomes a fool.

- When you have given nothing, ask for nothing.
- When you have no companion, look to your walking stick.
- Work like a slave and eat like a gentleman.
- You cannot hunt with a tied dog.

Algeria

- A friend is someone who shares your happiness and your pain.
- A secret for two is soon a secret for nobody.
- Cross the loud river but don't cross the silent one.
- Peace wins over wealth.
- The absent has always got a justification.
- The crow wanted to mimic the pigeon's walk and forgot his own.
- The hand which gives is better than the one which receives.
- The one who shows his fears ensures his salvation.
- Who got it, did get it; and who left it, did regret it.
- You know who your friend and your enemy are during difficult moments.
- Your eye is the only way you can judge thing.

Andorra

- As the old crow sing, so sings its fledglings.
- By perseverance everything reaches its target.
- Cast no dirt into the well that gives you water.
- He who hears no advice will not reach old age.
- Honey is sweet, but the bees sting.
- In times of famine no bread is stale.
- The best word is the unspoken word.
- Wisdom goes not always by years.
- With patience you go beyond knowledge.
- Women and cats in the house, men and dogs in the street.

Angola

- It is the voyage not the ship that matters.
- One spoon of soup in need has more value than a pot of soup when we have an abundance of food.
- The mysterious road beckons the young man.
- The one who throws the stone forgets; the one who is hit remembers forever.
- To be sure that your friend is a friend, you must go with him on a journey, travel with him day and night, go with him near and far.

Antigua and Barbuda

- Everything has its use.
- It is sometimes wisest to keep one's mouth shut.
- Use the right motivation for each person.
- Worrying does not improve a bad situation.
- Your actions and misdeeds will eventually have consequences.

Argentina

- A dog that barks all the time gets little attention.
- A false friend's tongue is sharper than a knife.
- A man who develops himself is born twice.
- Dress the monkey in silk and it is still a monkey.
- He who loves you will make you weep.
- If a man lends an ear, it's because he, too, wants to speak.
- If you have a tail of straw, then keep away from the fire.
- It's not the fault of the pig, but of the one who scratches his back.
- No woman can make a wise man out of a fool, but every woman can change a wise man into a fool.
- One door is shut, but a thousand are open.
- The larger the ship, the larger the storm.
- The one who loves you will also make you weep.
- The person that learns well also defends himself well.
- What is greatly desired is not believed when it comes.
- Woman is like your shadow; follow her, she flies; fly from her, she follows.

Armenia

- A mule can swim seven different strokes but the moment he sees the water he forgets them all.
- A pain in the foot is soon forgotten, a pain in the head is not.
- Advice is a gift that can become expensive for the one who gets it.
- As mills require two stones, so friendship requires two heads.
- Better to be an ant's head than a lion's tail.
- Choose a friend with the eyes of an old man, and a horse with the eyes of a young one.
- Clouds that thunder do not always rain.
- Dogs that fight each other will join forces against the wolf.
- Give a horse to the one who likes the truth so that on it he can escape.
- He who looks for a friend without a fault will never find one.
- He who speaks a lot learns little.
- If a rich man dies, all the world is moved; if a poor man dies, nobody knows it.
- If a woman hears that something unusual is going on in heaven, she would find a ladder to go and look.
- If you cannot become rich, be the neighbor of a rich man.
- It is better to carry stones with a wise man than accept the meal of a madman.
- To ask a favor from a miser is like trying to make a hole in water.
- Wealth can give legs to the cripple, beauty to the ugly, and

sympathy to tears.
- When asked "What news from the sea?" the fish replied; "I have a lot to say, but my mouth is full of water.".
- When they gave the donkey flowers to smell, he ate them.
- You cannot hit the point of a needle with a fist.

Australia

- A bad worker blames his tools.
- A bird in the hand is worth two in the bush.
- Don't count your chickens before they're hatched.
- Half a loaf is better than none.
- In the planting season visitors come singly, and in harvest time they come in crowds.
- None so deaf as those who would not hear.
- Once bitten, twice shy.
- The clash of ideas brings forth the spark of truth.
- Those who lose dreaming are lost.
- We are all visitors to this time, this place. We are just passing through.

Austria

- A blind chicken will often find an ear of corn.
- A light is still a light, even though the blind man cannot see it.
- Anyone who keeps the ability to see beauty never grows old.
- First bake the strudel then sit down and ponder.
- History is constantly teaching, but it does not find many pupils.
- If you shoot your arrows at stones, you will damage them.
- Imitate the sundial's ways, count only the pleasant days.
- Nothing ventured, nothing gained.
- Success has more than one father.
- The cripple is always the one to open the dancing.
- The earth does not shake when the flea coughs.
- What I do not know will not keep me warm.

Azerbaijan

- A mad man drops a rock into water well, so that thousand wise men cannot take it out.
- A man says his word to the face.
- A man would not lick what he spit.
- Beauty without virtue is a curse.
- Cheap meat never makes a good soup.
- Courage is ten, nine is the ability to escape.
- Courage mounted with occasion.
- Drop by drop would make a lake.
- Every tree casts shadow on its own bottom.
- Grass grows on its roots.
- Intelligence is in the head, not in the age.
- It's not shameful not to know, but it's shameful not to ask.
- Never mind storms and snows for the sake of a friend.
- One's own simple bread is much better than someone else's pilaf.
- Pass the bridge that your kinsmen have passed.
- Politeness is not sold in the bazaar.
- Smart bird gets trapped in its beak.
- Someone's end, someone's beginning.
- Speak not of what you have read, but about what you have understood.
- Until spring comes, nightingales do not sing.
- Without sowing a single wheat, you would not harvest thousand ones.

Bahamas

- A strawberry blossom will not sweeten dry bread.
- Cunning is superior to strength.
- Sickness accompanies a waning moon; a new moon cures disease.
- To engage in conflict, one does not bring a knife that cuts but a needle that sews.
- When the moon is not full, the stars shine more brightly.

Bahrain

- All you have is your nose, even if it's a bent one.
- Stretch your legs as far as your blanket.
- The world is in chaos, and the woman is looking for a partner.
- We taught them how to beg, then they beat us to the doorways.
- What's in the pan the spoon will dig out.
- Whoever doesn't reach the grapes, he says they're sour.
- You can't straighten a dog's tail.

Bangladesh

- A handful of love is better than an oven full of bread.
- A spared body only goes twenty-four hours further that another.
- As the master is away the workers take rest.
- At night one takes eels, it is worth waiting sometimes.
- Complete idiot who can keep silent, to a wise man is similar.
- Don't sell eggs in the bottom of hens.
- Even if two men remain on Earth, jealousy will reign.
- Flesh of man mends itself.
- Good remains are nice to have.
- Half-truth is more dangerous than falsehood.
- He who gets the grace of the women is neither hungry nor thirsty.
- Inside a well-nourished body, the soul remains longer.
- It is easier for the son to ask from the father than for the father to ask from the son.
- The more cowherds there are, the worse the cows are looked after.
- The one who does not make you happy when he arrives makes you happy when he leaves.
- The one who does not risk anything does not gain nor lose.
- There is no winter for who has remained in his mother's womb.
- To be poor is not a sin, it's better to avoid it anyway.
- To endure is obligatory, but to like is not.

- Wait for the night before saying that the day has been beautiful.
- When the poor man is buried, the large bell of the parish is silent.
- Who can master his thirst can master his health?
- Whose end of tongue is sharp, the edge of his head must be hard.

Barbados

- Excessive greed puts one in danger of losing everything.
- It is better to verify than to assume.
- Necessity or hard times forces people to do strange things.
- People of limited means can improve themselves by working together and combining resources.
- Seeing is different from having.
- Simple or minor annoyances may build up to cause major damage.
- Talking too much gets one in trouble.
- The more one shows off, the more one is vulnerable to ridicule and criticism.
- There's always a better lover than your current one.
- Unless you're close to someone you don't know the true nature of their problems.
- You are judged by the company you keep.
- Your reward or punishment is in line with your actions.

Belarus

- Fear the law not the judge.
- One who seeks no friends is his own enemy.
- We do not care of what we have, but we cry when it is lost.
- What makes you happy makes you rich.
- What the heart doesn't see the eyes will not see either.
- Who talks little hears better.

Belgium

- Children have a hair of their father.
- Don't make use of another's mouth unless it has been leant to you.
- Experience is the comb that nature gives us when we are bald.
- Experience is the father of wisdom.
- He who arrives too late finds the plate turned over.
- He who does not wish for little things does not deserve big things.
- It is no use waiting for your ship to come in unless you have sent one out.
- The horse must graze where it is tethered.
- Truth seldom finds a home.
- We have quite enough to do weeding our own garden.
- Weeds never perish.
- Who sieves too much keeps the rubbish.

Belize

- A friendship that dies is never reborn.
- Don't call the alligator a big-mouth till you have crossed the river.
- Don't carry all your eggs in one basket.
- Don't hang your hat higher than you can reach.
- If a man gives you a basket to carry water, it means that he hates you.
- Never drop the bone to catch the shadow.
- Remove the stone and you won't stumble.
- There is no use in wiping your butt before you defecate.

Benin

- A great affair covers up a small matter.
- Anyone who plants a tree before they die has not lived in vain.
- Anyone who sees beauty and does not look at it will soon be poor.
- Before you ask a man for clothes, look at the clothes that he is wearing.
- Blacksmiths and woodworkers will never suffer from poverty.
- Everyone has his place: the dead in the cemetery and the living at the table.
- Fear a silent man. He has lips like a drum.
- Many words do not fill a basket.
- The tortoise is friends with the snail: those with shells keep their shells close together.
- The world is a journey, the afterworld is home.
- The young cannot teach tradition to the old.
- We can only speak the truth when we turn off the light.
- What you give you get, ten times over.
- When the mouse laughs at the car, there is a hole nearby.
- Words are like spears: Once they leave your lips they can never come back.

Bhutan

- Clear the drain before it rains.
- Consider the tune, not the voice; consider the words, not the tune; consider the meaning, not the words.
- Flattering words will not be spoken from the mouth of an affectionate person.
- Fun and pleasure are located below the navel; dispute and trouble are also located there.
- If taken in excess, even mother's milk is poison.
- If the thought is good, the place and the path are good; if the thought is bad, the place and the path are bad.
- Never reveal all that you know to others. They might become shrewder than you.
- On the battlefield, there is no distinction between upper and lower class.
- The arrow of the accomplished master will not be seen when it is released; only when it hits the target.
- To give happiness to another person gives such a great merit; it cannot even be carried by a horse.
- To know your limitations is the hallmark of a wise person.
- Whatever joy you seek, it can be achieved by yourself; whatever misery you seek, it can be found by yourself.
- Words coming from far away are always half true, half false.
- You must first walk around a bit before you can understand the distance from the valley to the mountain.

Bolivia

- A quarrel is like buttermilk, the more you stir it, the sourer it grows.
- A thrashing river is a fisherman's bounty.
- He who marries prudence is the brother-in-law of peace.
- It is better to eat bread with love than fowl with grief.
- It's easier to know your enemies than to know your friends.
- Love and prudence are completely incompatible.
- Science makes men arrogant; wealth makes them fools.
- The beauty of the man is in his intelligence and the intelligence of the woman is in her beauty.

Bosnia and Herzegovina

- A brave man seldom is hurt in the back.
- Clean your own yard first before asking others to clean theirs.
- Don't be misled by the tears of a beggar.
- During the battle you cannot lend your sword to anyone.
- He who heeds the first word of his wife must listen forever to the second.
- One who lies for you will also lie against you.
- Two things rule the world, reward and punishment.
- When an ant gets wings, it loses its head.
- Why would you use poison if you can kill with honey?

Botswana

- A fool and water will go the way they are diverted.
- A lion cannot hear its own roar.
- A prudent man who knows proverbs, resolved problems.
- A slipshod man wastes away in the midst of plenty.
- All people share the same ancestry.
- Beautiful words don't put porridge in the pot.
- Do not look where the harvest is plentiful, but where the people are kind.
- If you live in a mud hut, beware of the rain.
- It is better to walk than curse the road.
- It is the one who lies by a fire who can feel how hot it is.
- Ninety-nine lies may help you, but the hundredth will give you away.
- One finger cannot pick up a louse.
- Only a dupe checks the depth of the water with both feet.
- Peace does not make a good ruler.
- Silence has a mighty noise.
- The earth is a termite mound, we all enter by the same opening.
- The fool is thirsty in the midst of water.
- The lice will roost on a dirty head.
- The lizard that lives high up in iroko tree does not hear the lions roar.

Brazil

- A sleeping fox finds no meat.
- A timely "no" beats a hasty "yes."
- Between the beginning and the end there is always a middle.
- Do not put the cart before the horse.
- For every ailing foot, there is a slipper.
- Goodwill makes the road shorter.
- He who knows nothing, doubts nothing.
- If it were ever to rain soup, the poor would only have forks.
- In the house of a blacksmith the ornaments are made of wood.
- Love is blind, so you have to feel your way.
- Never promise a poor person, and never owe a rich one.
- Never put off till tomorrow what you can do today.
- One who does not look ahead remains behind.
- Others will measure you with the same rod you use to measure them.
- Poverty is not a crime, but it's better not to show it.
- You cannot cover up the sun with a sieve.

Brunei

- Do not blame an uneven floor if you do not know how to dance.
- Do not think there are no crocodiles in still water.
- If you pinch your right thigh, your left thigh will feel it too.
- In a jungle with no lions, the blind monkey is king.
- Like the owl that misses the moon, a man wishes for the impossible.
- When elephants clash, the mousedeer dies in between
- When hearts fall out of favor, honey tastes like vinegar.
- Where there is grass, there are grasshoppers.

Bulgaria

- A crow will never be a dove.
- A person is known by the company he keeps.
- A word about to be spoken is like a stone that is ready to be thrown.
- An axe without a shaft is no threat to the forest.
- Bad weather gets better, a bad man never does.
- Bandage up your finger and take a walk in the village to see how many medical people you will meet.
- Eyes see everything but themselves.
- Grapes do not grow in a willow tree.
- Gravediggers have their own gravediggers too.
- He that feels sorry for the shoe, loses the horse.
- He that has a hawk has three hundred partridges.
- He that sleeps with a dog, should bear its fleas.
- He, who buys what he does not need, sells what he needs.
- Hunger is a bigger master than the king.
- If you are going to drown, do not try it in shallow water.
- If you can't be good, then be careful.
- If you cannot serve, you cannot rule.
- If you let everyone walk over you, then you become a carpet.
- If you want apples, you must shake the trees.
- Man is harder than a stone and more brittle than an egg.
- Many people wash their hands to have dinner with the bishop, only a few sit down to his table.
- The fox falls into the trap only once.

- Watch your step when you walk. You may find nothing, but you will not stumble.
- Where shepherds are lots, sheep are lost.
- With a king it is the same as with fire. Stay neither close by, nor too far away.

Burundi

- A rich man who does not know himself is worth less than a poor man who does.
- An elephant does not get tired carrying his trunk.
- Don't tell any more fairy tales when the child has gone to sleep.
- If you are dancing with your rivals, don't close your eyes.
- It is easy to pull a thorn out of someone else's skin.
- Nobody mourns an unnoticed death.
- Too many words blacken your ears.
- Where there is love there is no darkness.
- Who built the drum knows best what is inside.
- Without effort no harvest will be abundant.
- You can hide a mark on your skin, but not a defect.
- You cannot hide the smoke of the hut you set on fire.

Cambodia

- Cultivate a heart of love that knows no anger.
- Don't let an angry man wash dishes; don't let a hungry man guard rice.
- Don't reject the crooked road and don't take the straight one, instead take the one traveled by the ancestors.
- Don't shoot people you hate; don't lend to those you love.
- Don't take rich people as examples.
- For news of the heart ask the face.
- If you are patient in a moment of anger, you will spare yourself one hundred days of tears.
- If you know a lot, know enough to make them respect you, if you are stupid, be stupid enough so they can pity you.
- Negotiate a river by following its bends, enter a country by following its customs.
- People give, but don't be in a hurry to take.
- The boat sails by, the shore remains.
- The elephant that is stuck in the mud will tear down the tree with it.
- The immature rice stalk stands erect, while the mature stalk, heavy with grain, bends over.
- The tiger depends on the forest; the forest depends on the tiger.
- You don't have to cut a tree down to get at the fruit.

Cameroon

- A chattering bird builds no nest.
- He who asks questions, cannot avoid the answers
- If you do not step on the dog's tail, he will not bite you.
- Rain does not fall on one roof alone.
- A friend is worth more than a brother.
- Better a mistake at the beginning than at the end.
- Better little than too little.
- By trying repeatedly, the monkey learns how to jump from the tree.
- Every smart man is an ignoramus who abuses his ignorance.
- If everyone is going to dance, who, then, would watch?
- If love is a sickness, patience is the remedy.
- If the fight is tomorrow, then why should you clench your fist today?
- If the panther knew how much he is feared, he would do much more harm.
- It is better to be the victim of injustice than to be unjust yourself.
- No matter how fast a man is, he cannot outrun his shadow.
- One father can feed seven children, but seven children cannot feed one father.
- The darkness of night cannot stop the light of morning.
- The fire cannot be put out with your hands.
- What you don't know, you will not recognize.
- You cannot produce one human being without uniting two

bodies.

Canada

- Do not yell dinner until your knife is in the loaf.
- Patience is a tree whose root is bitter, but its fruit is very sweet.
- Walk a mile in my moccasins to learn where they pinch.
- When you talk about the sun, you will see her beams.
- You can't catch skunks with mice.

Chad

- A wasp can be more dangerous than a tiger.
- Every closed eye is not sleeping; and every open eye is not seeing.
- If you always walk down the same path, you'll go where you've already been.
- If you are tolerant in one moment of fury, you will prevent a year of regret.
- It's much easier to swim in the direction of the current.
- Laughter is a language everyone understands.
- Somewhere the sky touches the earth, and the name of that place is the end.
- The lion loves fish but hates wet feet.
- You are who you pretend to be.
- Your heart must be peaceful to hear song in the leaves of the trees.

Chile

- A bad rumor is better than bad news.
- Ambition spills the sack.
- Anguish is our worst advisor.
- He who divides and shares, always takes the best part.
- Never defecate more than what you eat.
- Never give thanks for a favor held back.
- No one has done good who has not suffered disillusionment.
- Where distrust enters, love is no more than a boy.

Colombia

- A lame man always speaks when it's time to run.
- All fear has much imagination and little talent.
- Better to beg forgiveness than to ask permission.
- Clean hands offend no one.
- He who overcomes his passions overcomes his greatest enemies.
- He who shows a passion tells his enemy where he may hit him.
- Instruction in youth is like engraving in stones.
- It's better to be the pot than the lid.
- Poverty does not destroy virtue nor wealth bestow it.
- See and believe, and in order not to make a mistake, touch.
- Suit the behavior to the occasion.
- Take the bull by the horns and the man at his word.
- The person who gives away his belongings will slowly become a beggar.
- The person who recognizes his major mistakes is on the road to wisdom.
- There is no better friend than a burden.
- To love and be wise is impossible.
- When force is imposed, the law is a joke.
- Who is always sad, does not even have fun when drunk.

Congo

- If the needle doesn't pass, the thread doesn't follow.
- Pride only goes the length one can spit.
- The teeth are smiling, but is the heart?
- Where there is no shame, there is no honor.
- You are beautiful; but learn to work, for you cannot eat your beauty.

Costa Rica

- A mind can make a heaven out of hell, or a hell out of heaven.
- All people have their friend and their enemy within themselves.
- Beauty and folly are constant companions.
- Envy shoots as others and wounds herself.
- Every word has three definitions and three interpretations.
- Once does not mean frequently, and twice does not mean constantly.
- The last to breathe is the first to drown.
- To give in order to receive is not to give, but to beg.

Croatia

- A good friend is worth more than a bad brother.
- A good horse has many faults; a bad one has hardly any.
- As soon as he set her down she said that she was tired.
- Better a bad harvest than a bad neighbor.
- Better be in debt than in shame.
- Check before you bite if it is bread or a stone.
- Don't measure a wolf's tail until he is dead.
- Even a dog will not eat a leg without flesh.
- Every bird has a hawk above it.
- Feed your horse as a friend, mount him as an enemy.
- If sorrow would not talk it would die.
- If you ask for too much at once, you will come home with an empty bag.
- If you take too long to choose, you will end up with the leftovers.
- It is better to be a bull for a year than a cow for a hundred years.
- It is better to work in your own land than to count your money abroad.
- No solutions without discussions.
- Save three pieces of gold and the fourth one will fall into your lap.
- The hunchback sees the hump of others, never his own.
- The starving man will never burn his bread.
- The udder of a neighbor's cow is always bigger.

- To follow everyone is wrong, to follow no one is worse.
- You may boast to strangers but tell the truth to your own people.

Cuba

- A lie runs until truth catches up to it.
- A love that can last forever takes but a second to come about.
- Cheese, wine, and a friend must be old to be good.
- Do not be excessively timid or excessively confident.
- Every head is a world.
- Faces of men we see but not their hearts.
- Gluttony and vanity grow with age.
- If you would be respected in company, seek the society of your equals and not of your superiors.
- Jovial companions make this dull life tolerable.
- Justice is a good thing, only not in my house, but in my neighbor's.
- Life is short; but it barely takes a second to smile.
- Listen to what they say about others, and you will know what they say about you.
- One washes the body in vain if one does not wash the soul.
- The best of hunters lies more than he hunts.
- The wise man never says, 'I did not think.'
- There is no better mirror than the face of an old friend.
- When the sun rises, it rises for everyone.

Czechia

- A crow sits next to a crow.
- After a battle, everyone is a general.
- Anger is the only thing to put off until tomorrow.
- Better a lie that soothes than a truth that hurts.
- Better to have a handful of might than a sack of justice.
- Blessed is the man who has friends, but woe to him who needs them.
- Do not choose your wife at a dance, but in the field among the harvesters.
- Good memories last long, bad ones last longer.
- He who cannot cut the bread evenly cannot get on well with people.
- He who digs a pit for other falls into it himself.
- He who is curious shall grow old soon.
- It is better not to begin than, having begun, leave unfinished.
- It is not the thief who is hanged, but one who was caught stealing.
- It is usually dark below the candlestick.
- No man has fallen from the sky learned.
- Our parents taught us to speak and the world taught us to be silent.
- The blacksmith's horse has no horseshoes.
- The fish does not go after the hook, but after the bait.
- The way one eats is the way one works.
- There can be no judge without an accused.

- Wait for a month before you praise a horse, and for a year before you praise a woman.
- What is called into a forest is the same what is echoed from the forest.
- When a man is not a lover in his twenties, not strong in his thirties, not rich in his forties and not wise in his fifties he will never be so.
- When the fool knows when to be silent, he would be sitting among the wise.
- Wisdom is easy to carry but difficult to gather.
- You will use in the old what you have learned young.

Denmark

- A child must creep until it learns to walk.
- A crowd is not company.
- A donkey that carries a lot of books is not necessarily learned.
- A friend's frown is better than a fool's smile.
- A good pilot is not known when the sea is calm and the weather fair.
- A good plan today is better than a perfect plan tomorrow.
- A little stone may upset a large cart.
- A slip of the foot may soon be recovered; but that of the tongue perhaps never.
- A willing helper does not wait until he is asked.
- A good neighbour is better than a brother far off.
- Age may wrinkle the face, but lack of enthusiasm wrinkles the soul.
- Ambition and revenge are always hungry.
- Bad is never good until worse happens.
- Better a little furniture than an empty house.
- Better a little in peace and with right, than much with anxiety and strife.
- Better ask twice than lose your way once.
- Blame is the lazy man's wages.
- Break one link and the whole chain falls apart.
- Joy is like the ague; one good day between two bad ones.
- Kind words don't wear out the tongue.
- Many have too much, but none enough.

- Speaking silence is better than senseless speech.
- The most difficult mountain to cross is the threshold.
- Where you cannot climb over, you must creep under.
- You may always find an opportunity in your sleeve, if you like.

Djibouti

- A dog does not mind being called a dog.
- A guest who breaks the dishes of his host is not soon forgotten.
- A lie has many variations, the truth none.
- A wound inflicted by a friend does not heal.
- Clouds do not always mean rain, but smoke is a sure sign of fire.
- The mighty tree falls, and the little birds scatter in the bush.
- The tears running down your face do not blind you.
- The wasp says that several regular trips to a mud pit enable it to build a house.
- What an adult sees from the ground, a boy cannot see even if he climbs a silk-cotton tree.

Dominican Republic

- A good surgeon must have a hawk's eye, a lion's heart and a woman's hand.
- Absence is the enemy of love; as the distance is from the eyes, so it is from the heart.
- Don't be like the shadow: a constant companion, yet not a comrade.
- If fate throws a knife at you, there are two ways of catching it: by the blade or by the handle.
- It is a fine thing to command, though it be only a herd of cattle.
- The devil always paints himself black, but we always see him rose-colored.
- The way of this world is to praise dead saints and persecute living ones.

Ecuador

- Anger of the mind is poison to the soul.
- Hands that give also receive.
- It's a fine sermon about fasting when the preacher just had lunch.
- No matter if the child's born with a flat nose, as long as it breathes.
- The devil's wiser more because of his age rather than being the devil.
- The strong forgive, the weak remember.

Egypt

- A beautiful thing is never perfect.
- A blow to another's purse is like a blow to a mountain of sand.
- A camel does not tease another camel about his humps.
- A man's ruin lies in his tongue.
- A monkey is a gazelle in its mother's eyes.
- An onion shared with a friend tastes like roast lamb.
- Cover your candle, it will light more.
- Error carries away the unteachable.
- For the benefit of the flowers, we water the thorns, too.
- Friendship doubles joy and halves grief.
- He who chatters with you will chatter about you.
- Honorable is the person who is aware of his power, yet refrains from inflicting bad things onto others.
- The barking of a dog does not disturb the man on a camel.
- The bullet that doesn't hit anything still makes a noise.
- The glow soon becomes ashes.
- The miser destroys what he collected.
- The opinion of the intelligent is better than the certainty of the ignorant.
- The tyrant is only the slave turned inside out.
- What comes easily is lost easily.
- When the angels present themselves, the devils abscond.
- Your friend chooses pebbles for you and your enemy counts your faults.

- Youth is beauty, even in cattle.

El Salvador

- Dip the pitcher into the water enough and it finally breaks.
- He who takes on too much squeezes little.
- It's fair that he who tried to steal yours, loses his.
- Say nothing about another that you wouldn't want to hear about yourself.
- So many years playing the marquise and she still doesn't know how to wave a fan.
- That which in the beautiful woman is grace, in the ugly woman turns to disgrace.

Estonia

- A much-used plow shines; stagnant waters stink.
- Barking dogs don't catch hares.
- Better a goat that can give milk than a cow that cannot.
- Earth is more precious than gold.
- Give good and get good.
- If the bread in the oven is a failure you lose a week; if the harvest is a failure you lose a year; if marriage is a failure, then you lose a life.
- If you go only once round the room, you are wiser than he who sits still.
- In a garment made of silk there are no fleas.
- Manure is the farmer's gold.
- Smart is the one who goes along with time, stupid is the one who bears his fangs.
- The mistakes of others are good teachers.
- The mouth is the interpreter for the heart.
- There is no room for two kings in one castle.
- When death comes, the rich man has no money and the poor man no debt.
- Where there is no fear, there is no pity.
- Who asks a lot will get wiser.
- Who cannot be trusted in small things cannot be trusted in big things.
- Who does not jump into water will not learn to swim.
- Who does not notice you in rags will not notice you in nice

clothes, who notices you in rags will also notice you in nice clothes.

- Who does not thank for a little will not thank for a lot.
- Who flees from a wolf will find a bear with two sons instead.
- Who has burnt himself with soup will blow on water as well.
- Who has not suffered from wounds will laugh at scars.
- Who is quick in youth will be diligent in old age.
- Who laughs early will cry later.
- Wise is who admits he is still ignorant.

Ethiopia

- A bird hanging between two branches will get bitten on both wings.
- A blade won't cut another blade; a cheat won't cheat another cheat.
- A fool looks for dung where the cow never browsed.
- A home without a woman is like a barn without cattle.
- As the wound inflames the finger, so the thought inflames the mind.
- Better an egg this year than a chicken next year.
- Cactus is bitter only to him who tastes it.
- Confiding a secret to an unworthy person is like carrying a grain in a bag with a hole in it.
- Dine with a stranger but save your love for your family.
- Do not hesitate or you will be left in between doing something, having something and being nothing.
- Eat when the food is ready; speak when the time is right.
- It is better to be the cub of a live jackal than of a dead lion.
- It is foolhardy to start a fire just to see the flames.
- It is foolish for someone to remain thirsty when he is in the midst of water.
- One should punish a child the first time he comes home with a stolen egg. Otherwise, the day he returns home with a stolen ox, it will be too late.
- Restless feet may walk into a snake pit.
- The cattle is as good as the pasture in which it grazes.

- The cow knows the cowherd but not the owner.
- The person who grew up without correction will find his mouth slipping instead of his foot.
- The same water never runs into the same river.
- The slimming of an elephant and the losses of a rich man are not noticeable.
- What one desires is always better than what one has.
- When spiders unite, they can tie down a lion.
- When the heart overflows, it comes out through the mouth.
- Who cannot yet walk, cannot climb a ladder.
- Woman without man is like a field without seed.

Faroe Islands

- A crow likes her own chick the best.
- After a landslide one more can be expected.
- An eager dog often gets a torn skin.
- As we are egged on, we rage.
- Better be a good man's slave than badly married.
- Big rivers are made of many small brooks.
- Blind is the bookless man.
- Everything is better than owning nothing.
- Haste often causes nasty things.
- He that rows out often, gets fish at last.
- He who waits gets a tailwind, and he who rows, a harbor.
- Hear about others but make it cozy for yourselves.
- It's better to be prepared than swift afterwards.
- It's difficult to build a boat plank against the wave.
- None reaches further than his arms reach.
- Nothing ventured, nothing won.
- Small fish are better than empty dishes.
- The one who derides others, gets derided too.
- The thief believes that everybody steals.
- Time runs like the river current.
- We are born to be our own, and not fed to it.
- When ale goes in, the wit goes out.
- When the mouse is full, the flour tastes bitter.
- You can take the ox to the river but begging it won't make it drink.

Finland

- A child is like an axe; even if it hurts, you still carry them on your shoulders.
- A small candle can light up the darkest forest.
- A spot in gold and a fault in a wise man are soon visible.
- Age does not give sense it only makes one go slowly.
- Don't beat the man who has already been beaten.
- Even a small star shines in the darkness.
- Even the crow sings with its own voice.
- From a word comes a word; from a spark the earth catches fire.
- Help a man uphill, not at the foot of the hill.
- If a man knew where he would fall, he would spread straw there first.
- One who grows up without discipline will die without glory.
- One year ages the old, two years grow a child.
- The cat would eat fish, too, but it wouldn't jump into the ocean.
- The mouth brought the wolf into the trap, the tongue the ermine to the snare.
- The woman should let the man lead the dance.
- War does not determine who is right, only who is remaining.

Fiji

- Each bay, its own wind.
- Idleness is to be dead at the limbs but alive within.
- Life is like this: sometimes sun, sometimes rain.

France

- Better to anticipate than to heal.
- Better to be alone than accompanied badly.
- Dogs don't make cats.
- Everyone sees noon at their door.
- It's not as if you must drink the sea.
- Little by little, the bird builds its nest.
- The night carries advice.
- The outfit doesn't make the monk.
- There are only imbeciles who don't change their opinions.
- To a good cat, a good rat.
- Who will live, will see.
- You don't teach an old monkey how to make funny faces.
- You should turn your tongue around in your mouth seven times before you speak.

Gabon

- A single stick may smoke but it will not burn.
- Bad friends will prevent you from having good friends.
- Even if thin, the elephant remains the king of the forest.
- Living is worthless for one without a home.

Gambia

- A fly that has no one to advice it, follows the corpse into the grave.
- An adult squatting sees farther than a child on top of tree.
- Before healing others, heal yourself.
- Giant silk cotton trees grow out of very tiny seeds.
- However black a cow is, the milk is always white.
- If a child's hands are clean, he can eat with elders.
- If a donkey kicks you and you kick back, you are both donkeys.
- No matter how long a log may float in the water, it will never become a crocodile.

Georgia

- Better your own copper than another man's gold.
- Beware of the front of a bull, the back of a horse and both sides of a blind man.
- Catch the bird before you build a cage.
- Do not blame the sun for the darkness of the night.
- Give a blind man eyes and he will ask for eyebrows.
- He who is in a hurry always arrives late.
- If you forgive the fox for stealing your chickens, he will take your sheep.
- If you give a man nuts, then give him something to crack them with.
- In a place without dogs they teach the cats to bark.
- One dirty pig pollutes others.
- The buzzing of the flies does not turn them into bees.
- The rich eat when they want, the poor when they can.
- The tall one wouldn't bend; the short one wouldn't stretch, and the kiss was lost.
- When they came to milk the cow, she said "I am an ox", and when they came to harness her she said "I am a cow".
- When you put your nose into the water your cheeks get wet as well.
- You can better drink from a small well with soft water than from the salty sea.

Germany

- Actions say more than words.
- All beginnings are hard.
- Appetite emerges while eating.
- Crooked logs also make straight fires.
- Don't worry about eggs that haven't been laid yet.
- Failure makes smart.
- First think, then act.
- He who chases two rabbits at once will catch none.
- He who rests grows rusty.
- He who says A also has to say B.
- Honesty lasts the longest.
- If the rider is no good, it's the horse's fault.
- Make haste with leisure.
- One certainty is better than ten uncertainties.
- Practice is what makes a master.
- Starting is easy, persistence is an art.
- The cheapest is always the most expensive.
- The devil's favorite piece of furniture is the long bench.
- The morning hour has gold in its mouth.
- Work is work and liquor is liquor.
- You don't see the forest for all the trees.
- You have to take things the way they come.
- Yourself is the man.

Ghana

- A child does not laugh at the ugliness of his mother.
- A crab does not beget a bird.
- A cracked bell can never sound well.
- A slave does not choose his master.
- By going and coming, a bird weaves its nest.
- By the time the fool has learned the game, the players have dispersed.
- Death has the key to open the miser's chest.
- Do not call the forest that shelters you a jungle.
- Don't expect to be offered a chair when you visit a place where the chief himself sits on the floor.
- He who seems to be for you may be working against you.
- If an opportunity is not taken when it comes, it passes away.
- If two selfish young men sit next to a pot of water, the water spills out on the ground.
- If youthful pride were wealth, then every man would have had it in his lifetime.
- It is not wrong to go back for that which you have forgotten.
- No one tests the depth of the river with both feet.
- One camel does not make fun of another camel's hump.
- People working on the slope of a mountain do not look at the buttocks of one another.
- The left-hand washes the right and the right washes the left.
- The prickly branches of the palm tree do not show preference even to friends.

- The rain wets the leopard's spots but does not wash them off.
- The responsibility of power is like holding an egg. Grasp it too tightly and it will drip through your fingers; hold it too loosely and it will drop and break.
- The ruin of a nation begins in the homes of its people.
- We must go back and reclaim our past, so we can move forward; so we understand why and how we came to be who we are today.
- When a deceiving man tells you to climb a tree, tell him to climb it first. If he finds a comfortable spot you can follow him.
- When a king has good counsellors, his reign is peaceful.

Greece

- From outside the dance-circle, you sing a lot of songs.
- Many words is poverty.
- My home, my little home, a little house of my own.
- People who do not see each other frequently, they soon forget each other.
- The camel doesn't see her own hump.
- The donkey called the rooster big headed.
- The tongue has no bones, but bones it crushes.
- Too many opinions sink the boat.
- Unripe grape gets sweet as honey, at a slow pace.
- When the cat is away, the mice dance.

Guatemala

- A weapon is an enemy even to its owner.
- Better to eat beans in peace than to eat meat in distress.
- Do not bear ill will toward those who tell you the truth.
- Don't despise someone for telling the truth.
- Everyone is the age of their heart.
- He who avoids the temptations avoids the sin.
- He who doesn't risk a penny doesn't make a peso.
- It's not the fault of the parrot, but of the one who teaches him to talk.
- Return property to its owner, and your sleep will be peaceful.
- That which is said at the table should be wrapped up in the tablecloth.
- The deepest waters make the least noise.
- There's no ill that doesn't turn out for the better.
- Your true enemy lives in your own house.

Guinea

- A cow that has no tail should not try to chase away flies.
- A good deed is something one returns.
- Around a flowering tree, there are many insects.
- For news of the heart, ask the face.
- He who has done evil, expects evil.
- He who has not yet reached the opposite shore should not make fun of him who is drowning.
- He, who does not cultivate his field, will die of hunger.
- Knowledge is like a garden: if it is not cultivated, it cannot be harvested.
- No matter how long the winter, spring is sure to follow.
- Save your fowl before it stops flapping.
- The man on his feet carries off the share of the man sitting down.
- The man who builds his own throne rules over a desert.
- The man who can't dance says the band can't play.
- The toad likes water, but not when it's boiling.
- To have two eyes can be cause for pride; but to have one eye is better than to have none.
- To make preparations does not spoil the trip.
- When a needle falls into a deep well, many people will investigate the well, but few will be ready to go down after it.
- When you wait for tomorrow it never comes. When you don't wait for it tomorrow still comes.

Guyana

- Always be prepared for the worst.
- Don't make fun of circumstances that could one day be your own.
- Don't wait until it's too late to see things when there have been clear warnings.
- If you don't want to heed advice or warning, you must bear the consequences.
- It's too easy to use ignorance as an excuse for our mistakes.
- Just a bit of evidence can tell you a lot.
- Treat all children the way you would treat your own.
- When you are too kind to people, they will take advantage.
- When you hurt one family member, it hurts the whole family.
- When you tell one person a secret, it is bound to spread.

Haiti

- A beautiful funeral doesn't guarantee heaven.
- A borrowed drum never makes good dancing.
- A little dog is brave in front of his master's house.
- A monkey never thinks her baby's ugly.
- A mother never bites her child to the bone.
- A protector is like a cloak.
- An empty sack can't stand up.
- If work were a good thing the rich would have grabbed it a long time ago.
- If you want to catch a wild horse, find a tight corral.
- Just because someone is smiling at you doesn't mean they're your friend.
- People talk and don't act.
- Remember the rain that made your corn grow.
- Roaches are never right when facing chickens.
- Smelling good is expensive.
- That which doesn't kill you makes you fat.
- The constitution is paper, bayonets are steel.
- Wife for a time, mother for all time.
- You know how to run, but you don't know how to hide.

Honduras

- Choose the stone by the size of the frog.
- Every time one laughs a nail is removed from one's coffin.
- For great ills, great remedies.
- For the lazy and the poor, everything always takes twice the effort.
- Grief shared is half grief; Joy shared is double joy.
- He who walks the path of evil comes upon an evil end.
- Hunger has no law; it's just hungry.
- No matter if the child's born blind, as long as it doesn't beg.
- The truth is bitter and lies are sweet.
- When the blind leads the way, woe to those who follow.

Hungary

- A good priest learns till he dies.
- A mug keeps going to the well until it breaks eventually.
- Appearance cheats sometimes.
- Even the blind chicken finds grains.
- Even walls have ears.
- Expect good for a good deed.
- Lots of small will amount to a lot.
- Misery loves company.
- One swallow does not make a summer.
- Practice makes perfect.
- Strike while the iron is hot.
- The bushes don't rattle if there's no wind.
- The exception strengthens the rule.
- The horse has four legs and still stumbles.
- The smart one will learn from the mistakes of others.
- There are as many customs as houses.
- They catch up with a liar sooner than with a limping dog.
- Time is money.
- Unwillingness ends in groaning.
- Who doesn't appreciate the little does not deserve the big.

Iceland

- A bad rower blames his oars.
- Bake while the fire burns.
- Blind is a man without a book.
- He who has thrown fish overboard, may well fast.
- Invalid are the words of minors.
- It is a friend who warns.
- It is late to fence in the well when the child has fallen into it.
- Looks do not decide the good qualities.
- Many are difficult to see through.
- Many go to a goats' house to ask for wool.
- No one is excessively stupid if he can keep silent.
- One thing is luck, another thing ability.
- Similar children play best together.
- The gift expects another gift in return.
- Things look bleak for the one who lives in a foreign country.
- Those who are considered good, resemble each other in much.
- Those who get praised most loudly, disappoint me the most.

India

- A known mistake is better than an unknown truth.
- A mother is a school, preparing her is like preparing a good nation.
- Advice sharpens a rusty opinion.
- Among the blind, the one-eyed man is king.
- Better a hundred enemies outside the house than one inside.
- Better to have a diamond with a few small flaws than a rock that is perfect.
- Complaining is the weak man's weapon.
- Dependence on another is perpetual disappointment.
- Don't bargain for fish which are still in the water.
- Fish and guests smell when they are three days old.
- He who has a true friend, has no need of a mirror.
- If you are up to your knees in pleasure, then you are up to your waist in grief.
- It is little use to dig a well after the house has caught fire.
- Learning is a treasure no thief can touch.
- One and one sometimes make eleven.
- One finger can't lift a pebble.
- Pearls are of no value in a desert.
- Smiles that you broadcast, will always come back to you.
- Something done at the wrong time should be regarded as not done.
- Speak like a parrot; meditate like a swan; chew like a goat; and bathe like an elephant.

- The eyes do not see what the mind does not want.
- The worst kind of poverty is to have many debts.
- True happiness lies in giving it to others.
- Where the needle goes, the thread follows.
- You can often find in rivers what you cannot find in oceans.
- You do not stumble over a mountain, but you do over a stone.

Indonesia

- A bad workman blames his tools.
- A friend in need is a friend indeed.
- A good marksman may miss, the pitcher goes so often to the well that it is broken at last.
- A penny saved is a penny gained.
- Better an egg today than a hen tomorrow.
- Birds of feather flock together.
- Do not bite off more than you can chew.
- Do not judge a book by its cover.
- Every why has its wherefore.
- Leaves do not wave if there is no wind.
- Life is what you make of it.
- Look before you leap, because snakes among sweet flowers do creeps.
- Misery loves company.
- No pain no gain.
- The rotten apple spoils the whole barrel.
- What goes around comes around.
- Where there is a will, there is a way.

Iran

- A drowning man is not bothered by rain.
- A fool's excuse is bigger than his mistake.
- A greedy man is always poor.
- A quality statement often gets no answer.
- A single rose does not mean that it is spring.
- A stone thrown at the right time is better than gold given at the wrong time
- A sword in the hands of a drunken slave is less dangerous than science in the hands of the immoral.
- A timely tear is better than a misplaced smile.
- An egg thief becomes a camel thief.
- Curiosity is the key to knowledge.
- Do little things now; and big things will come to you.
- Excessive praise is like an insult.
- It's better to flee and stay alive than to die and become a hero.
- Marriage is an uncut watermelon.
- Necessity can change a lion into a fox.
- Solved riddles look easy.
- The night hides a world but reveals a universe.
- The way a house is decorated will tell much about its owner.
- Thinking is the essence of wisdom.
- You can close the city gates, but you can't close the people's mouths.
- You can't pick up two watermelons with one hand.

Iraq

- A book is like a garden carried in the pocket.
- All authors should prepare to encounter criticism.
- An army of sheep led by a lion would defeat an army of lions led by a sheep.
- He who can't manage his wheat himself will eat his barely.
- If you conduct yourself properly, then fear no one.
- One who is drowning will even grab onto a snake.
- Someone who does not know how to dance says the ground is sloping.
- Sometimes you need to sacrifice your beard in order to save your head.
- The provision for tomorrow belongs to tomorrow.
- You can have a lord, you can have a king, but the man to fear is the tax collector.
- You do not exit the hammam the same as you entered.
- You will discover your true friends in moments of crisis.

Ireland

- A blind man is no judge of colors.
- A friend's eye is a good mirror.
- A good word never broke a tooth.
- A man's mouth often breaks his nose.
- An awkward colt often becomes a beautiful horse.
- Any man can lose his hat in a fairy wind.
- Better to spend money like there's no tomorrow than spend tonight like there's no money.
- Beware of the anger of a patient man.
- Complain that you have no shoes until you meet a man who has no feet.
- Do not take the thatch from your own roof to buy slates for another man's house.
- Even black hens lay white eggs.
- Every man is sociable until a cow invades his garden.
- Every patient is a doctor after his cure.
- Hindsight is the best insight to foresight.
- If you are looking for a friend without a fault you will be without a friend forever.
- It is better to be a coward for a minute than dead for the rest of your life.
- It's not a delay to stop and sharpen the scythe.
- Life is like a cup of tea; it's all in how you make it.
- No matter how many rooms you have in your house, you're only able to sleep in one bed.

- Show the fatted calf but not the thing that fattened him.
- The cat is always dignified until the dog comes by.
- The older the fiddle the sweeter the tune.
- The skin of the old sheep is on the rafter no sooner than the skin of the young sheep.
- There was never a scabby sheep in a flock that didn't like to have a comrade.
- When the apple is ripe, it will fall.
- You must crack the nuts before you can eat the kernel.
- You'll never plough a field by turning it over in your mind.

Israel

- A bird that you set free may be caught again, but a word that escapes your lips will not return.
- A cheerful heart is good medicine, but a crushed spirit dries up the bones.
- A pessimist, confronted with two bad choices, chooses both.
- A slave shows his true character, not while he is enslaved but when he becomes a master.
- Ask about your neighbors, then buy the house.
- Commit a sin twice and it will not seem a crime.
- God could not be everywhere, and therefore he made mothers.
- He who puts up with insult invites injury.
- If the rich could hire someone else to die for them, the poor would make a wonderful living.
- If there is bitterness in the heart, sugar in the mouth won't make life sweeter.
- Never trust the man who tells you all his troubles but keeps from you all his joys.
- One of life's greatest mysteries is how the boy who wasn't good enough to marry your daughter can be the father of the smartest grandchild in the world.
- Time heals old pain, while it creates new ones.
- We do not see things the way they are but as we are.
- What one has, one doesn't want, and what one wants, one doesn't have.

- What you don't see with your eyes, don't invent with your mouth.
- When a father gives to his son, both laugh; when a son gives to his father, both cries.
- When you're hungry, sing; when you're hurt, laugh.
- Where two Jews, three opinions.
- Worries go down better with soup.
- You can't force anyone to love you or lend you money.

Italy

- A candle loses nothing by lighting another candle.
- A favor to come is better than a hundred received.
- A forced kindness deserves no thanks.
- Anger can be an expensive luxury.
- Better give a penny then lend twenty.
- Better one day as a lion than a hundred as a sheep.
- Between saying and doing many a pair of shoes is worn out.
- Every rule has an exception.
- He who begins many things finishes but few.
- He who does not when he can, cannot when he will.
- He who does nothing, does not fail.
- He who finds a friend, finds a treasure.
- People in glass houses should not throw stones.
- Silence gives consent.
- The habit doesn't make a monk.
- The liar needs a good memory.
- Trouble rides a fast horse.
- Who offends writes on sand; who is offended, on marble.
- Wise men learn by other men's mistakes, fools by their own.

Ivory Coast

- A bad son gives his mother a bad name.
- A friend will wipe away sweat but not blood.
- A poor man's sheep will never get fat.
- Better a bad wife than an empty house.
- Everybody loves a fool, but nobody wants him for a son.
- He who cannot sleep can still dream.
- In the village that you don't know, the chickens have teeth.
- In the villages where there are no oxen, the sheep's feet seem strong.
- Ingratitude is sooner or later fatal to its author.
- Mutual affection is when each gives his share.
- Taking aim for too long can ruin your eyes.
- Taking water from the same well doesn't make all the wives' gravy taste good.
- Teeth will never quarrel with the tongue.
- The death of an elderly man is like a burning library.
- The panther and the sheep never hunt together.
- The twig that falls in the water will never become a fish.
- Two flavors confuse the palate.
- Until the snake is dead, do not drop the stick.

Jamaica

- A bird cannot fly with one wing.
- A blind man sees his neighbor's faults.
- A cockroach has no business in a fowl fight.
- A drunken man speaks the truth.
- A tailor never owns an expensive suit.
- Do not allow your right hand to know what your left hand does.
- Do not count your chicken before they are hatched.
- Don't throw away your stick before you cross the river.
- If a black fowl is not yours, you will call him a vulture.
- It is not every rainfall that should wet you.
- Never bite the hands that feed you.
- One cannot take a cow's tail to fry its own skin.
- Showing off will bring disgrace.
- You cannot sow corn seeds and expect to reap peas.

Japan

- A bad wife is 100 years of crop failure.
- A frog in a well does not know the great sea.
- A journey of a thousand miles begins with the first step.
- After the rain, the earth hardens.
- After victory, tighten your helmet strap.
- Alcohol reveals true feelings.
- Fall seven times, stand up eight.
- If you take shade, do it under a large tree.
- Many skills is no skill.
- Nothing is more expensive than free.
- Perseverance is power.
- Pleasure seekers have no free time.
- Similar types call each other friends.
- Suspicion will raise bogies.
- Ten men, ten colors.
- The prime of your life does not come twice.
- The stake that stands out is struck.
- Unless an idiot dies, he won't be cured.
- Watch a person's behavior and correct your own behavior.
- With many little strokes a large tree is felled.

Jordan

- A promise is a cloud; fulfillment is rain.
- Do not cut down the tree that gives you shade.
- Do not tell a friend anything you would conceal from an enemy.
- If destiny does not fit you, fit yourself to destiny.
- In the desert of life, the wise person travels by caravan, while the fool prefers to travel alone.
- Laugh, and the world laughs with you; weep, and you weep alone.
- Sometimes coincidence is better than a thousand meetings.

Kazakhstan

- A wolf cannot get enough of sheep and a man cannot get enough of thinking.
- Even a mole feels strong when it is in his hole.
- Happiness does not run away from the people and craftiness cannot slip away from the people.
- If a horse misses its herd, it stamps its back hooves. If a man misses company, he harnesses his horse.
- One can live with loss of sight but cannot live without people.
- People's smile is hotter than the sun.
- To go up against people is like to swim against the current.
- Who leads the people will swallow butter, who lags behind the people will swallows dust.

Kenya

- A rat-trap catches both the guilty and the innocent.
- A rope parts where it is thinnest.
- A sinking ship doesn't need a captain.
- A word in the heart does not win.
- All monkeys cannot hang on the same branch.
- An empty pot makes the loudest noise.
- An orphaned calf licks its own back.
- At the harvest, you know how good the millet is.
- Because a man has injured your goat, do not go out and kill his bull.
- Crawling on hands and knees has never prevented anyone from walking upright.
- Do not say the first thing that comes to your mind.
- He who does not know one thing knows another.
- He who refuses to obey cannot command.
- Hurrying has no blessing.
- Intelligence is like hair, everyone has his own.
- It is better for the eye to die than the heart.
- It is better to be poor when one is young, rather than becoming poor at old age.
- It is the grass that suffers when elephants fight.
- No matter how tall the neck is, the head will always be on top of it

Kiribati

- A great leader is like the rain that calms the ocean.
- A man is who he is by his own making, not as a result of another's work.

Korea

- A rolling stone extracts a stone that is embedded.
- A rolling stone gathers no moss.
- A widower knows a widow's sorrow.
- Ask first then go, even if it's a road you know.
- Beauty is in the eye of the beholder.
- Birds hear the words spoken in the day, and mice hear the words spoken at night.
- Delight comes at the end of difficulty.
- Even a worm will wiggle if you step on it
- Even if the sky collapses, there is a hole to escape out of
- Even though a tiger is biting you, if you gain consciousness, you can live.
- First knock on the stone bridge before crossing.
- If going words are beautiful, coming words will be beautiful.
- If it becomes distant from your eyes, it also becomes distant from your heart.
- If you lift together, it's better even if it's a sheet of paper.
- Laughter is the best healer.
- The start is the half.
- There is a time when even a monkey falls from a tree.
- There is no shortcut to learning.
- You can know a promising tree from when it's a baby tree.
- You can lead a horse and go to a stream, but you can't make it drink water through its own will.

Kyrgyzstan

- A bird trusts itself, a dog trusts its master.
- A friend looks at your eyes, an enemy looks at your feet.
- A good wife is half of happiness in your life.
- If your right hand is angry, hold it back with your left.
- Knowledge builds up, ignorance destroys.
- The earth is a small place for fugitives.

Laos

- Although he who walks behind an elephant may feel very secure, he is likely to get splattered with elephant dung.
- Learning means loving the country.
- When the water rises, the fish eat the ants; when the water falls, the ants eat the fish.
- You know, you teach. You do not know, you learn.

Latvia

- "We have rowed well," said the flea as the fishing boat arrives at its mooring.
- A good backside will easily find a bench to sit on.
- A strange glass is emptied in one draught; your own glass not even in ten.
- As long as you live, you learn.
- Every man forges his own destiny.
- If you can't use your eyes, follow your nose.
- In dense woods the trees grow straight.
- Let the devil into church and he will climb into the pulpit.
- Never wrestle with a strong man nor bring a rich man to court.
- No matter how much you eat, save some seeds for sowing.
- On the hook of truth only small carp will bite; in the net of falsehood the big salmon are caught.
- Once you've cut the bread, you cannot put it together again.
- Promised berries will not fill the basket.
- Sleep is the poor man's treasure.

Lebanon

- A bite from a loving mouth is worth more than a kiss from any other.
- A cemetery never refuses a corpse.
- A clear conscience shines not only in the eyes.
- A dog will always be a dog, even if he is raised by lions.
- Good advice once was worth a camel; now that it is free of charge, no one takes it.
- Have faith in a stone and you will be healed by it.
- He who gossips to you will gossip about you.
- He who has money can eat ice cream in hell.
- If a rich man eats a snake, people call it wisdom; if a poor man does the same thing, people call it derangement.
- If anyone is not willing to accept your point of view, try to see his point of view.
- If someone puts their trust in you, don't sever it.
- If you follow the lead of the cockerel, you'll be led to the poulter.
- Lock your door rather than suspect your neighbor.
- Lower your voice and strengthen your argument.
- No one can give what he does not have.
- Only your nail scratches your skin.
- Some men will build a wine cellar when they have found just one grape.
- The person who knew you when you were young will seldom respect you as an adult.

- Two things cannot be hidden: being astride a camel and being pregnant.
- When a mouse makes fun of a cat, there is a hole nearby.
- When the angels arrive, the demons leave.
- When you come back from a trip bring something for the family, even if it is only a stone.
- You cannot cook your eggs with wind

Lesotho

- A farmer who doesn't work in the rain or under the sun has nothing to harvest at the end of the farming year.
- An elephant does not die of one broken rib.
- Cattle are born with ears; their horns grow later.
- Youths talk first and then listen; the elderly listen and then talk.

Liberia

- A little rain each day will fill the rivers to overflowing.
- Do not eat your chicken and throw its feathers in the front yard.
- Do not look where you fell, but where you slipped.
- Don't look where you fell, but where you slipped.
- Good millet is known at the harvest.
- If the townspeople are happy, look for the chief.
- If the walls were adamant; gold would take the town.
- Only when the tree is big and strong can you tether a cow to it.
- Though the palm tree in the jungle is big, who knows how big its yield will be?
- To the patient man will come all the riches of the world.
- When building a house, don't measure the timbers in the forest.

Libya

- As long as a human being lives, he will learn.
- If you plant olives but do not prune the tree, your oil will be good for only donkeys.
- Maliciously acquired gold never lasts long.
- Silence is the door of consent.
- Women were born to be treasured.

Liechtenstein

- Charity sees the need not the cause.
- He who borrows sells his freedom.
- He who conquers his anger has conquered an enemy.
- He who wants to warm himself in old age must build a fireplace in his youth.
- Speaking comes by nature, silence by understanding.

Lithuania

- A name does not ruin the thing itself.
- A shoe-maker walks barefooted.
- Crows will not pick other crows' eyes.
- The king searches for a crumb.
- To be without learning, is to be without eyes.
- To be without learning, is to be without eyes.
- We all are brothers-in-law.
- You must get your son, your wife and your bread from your native village.

Luxembourg

- A man's eyes are for seeing, a woman's for being seen.
- A woman is as old as she wants to tell you she is.
- A woman is as old as she wishes to tell you.
- A woman is at her strongest when she faints.
- A woman who likes to wash will find water.
- In the eyes of its mother every turkey is a swan.
- Keep your eye on girls that don't tell their mothers everything.
- The wife cries before the wedding, the husband after.
- Truth is what women do not tell.
- Words are but dwarfs, examples are giants.
- Your wife and your wheelbarrow are two things that you should never lend to anyone.

Macedonia (FYROM)

- A bear that dances in your neighbor's house might soon dance in yours.
- A good friend is recognized in times of trouble.
- Enjoy yourself, for there is nothing in the world we can call our own.
- Feed a dog to bark at you.
- If my neighbor is happy, my own work will go easier, too.
- The brain is not in the pocket, but in the head.
- Think twice, say once.
- Where force rules, justice does not exist.

Madagascar

- All who live under the sky are woven together like one big mat.
- Like the chameleon, one eye on the future, one eye on the past.
- People are like plants in the wind: they bow down and rise up again.
- Truth is like sugar cane; even if you chew it for a long time, it is still sweet.
- Without the forest, there will be no more water, without water, there will be no more rice.
- You can't catch a louse with one finger.

Malawi

- Buffaloes are held by ropes, man by his words.
- Clapping with the right hand only will not make a noise.
- Do not be like the mosquito that bites the owner of the house.
- Don't teach the tiger cub to eat meat.
- Don't think there are no crocodiles just because the water's calm.
- Gold is a debt we can repay, but kindness not till our dying day.
- However big the whale may be, the tiny harpoon can rob him of life.
- One finger cannot crush a louse.
- The betrothed of good is evil; the betrothed of life is death; the betrothed of love is divorce.
- There is no difference between mother and baby snakes, they are equally poisonous.
- We are born from the womb of our mother; we are buried in the womb of the earth.
- Wisdom is like mushrooms that come after you have finished eating.
- You can measure the depth of the sea but what about a man's heart?

Malaysia

- Do not be tricked into thinking that there are no crocodiles just because the water is still.
- Don't think there are no crocodiles because the water's calm.
- Don't use an axe to embroider.
- Fear to let fall a drop and you will spill a lot.
- Feasting is the physician's harvest.
- If you are too shy to ask, you might lose your way. When you go away, the conversation changes.
- If you plant grass, you won't get rice.
- No matter how big the whale is, a tiny harpoon can kill him.
- The body pays for a slip of the foot, and gold pays for a slip of the tongue.
- To truly love your wife, leave her alone every once in a while.

Mali

- A deaf man may not have heard the thunder, but he surely will see the rain.
- A man is what he thinks.
- A turtle is not proud of his long neck.
- A woman who offers sex to everyone will get kicked by everyone.
- If you've nothing to do, dig a spinster's grave.
- Life is like a ballet performance, danced only once.
- Slowly but surely the excrement of foreign poets will come to your village.
- The hyena chasing two antelopes at the same time will go to bed hungry.
- When mosquitoes work, they bite and then they sing.
- You cannot wage war without the sound of gunpowder.
- You must decide where you are going in the evening, if you intend to leave early in the morning.
- You will never drown where you always take a bath.

Malta

- Better an ache than a tear.
- Death is the only thing that's certain.
- Do not bandage your head before you break it.
- Don't buy fish in the sea.
- He who waits patiently is rewarded.
- The cat and the rat never thought alike.
- The legs go where the heart is.
- The liar has a short lifespan.
- The question is the sister of wisdom.
- Trust the words of the old man.
- We are all made of flesh and blood.
- What was is no more, what if is just if.

Mauritania

- A cutting word is worse than a bowstring; a cut may heal, but the cut of the tongue does not.
- A stone from the hand of a friend is an apple.
- Before eating, open thy mouth.
- He who begins a conversation, does not foresee the end.
- He who has no spoon will burn his hands.
- He who loves money must labor.
- He who wears too fine clothes, shall go about in rags.
- He whose clothes are too fine, shall go about in rags.
- If you watch your pot, your food will not burn.
- It is only the water that is spilled; the bowl is not broken.
- Not all the flowers of a tree produce fruit.
- Not all the tree's blossoms will bear fruit.
- One must talk little and listen a lot.
- Open your mouth before you eat.
- Too large a morsel chokes the child.
- Two eyes see better than one.

Mexico

- A dog that does not go out does not find the bone.
- A steady step is better than a run that tires.
- Actions speak louder than words.
- Be careful what you wish for as it could become true.
- Better alone than poorly accompanied.
- Better late than never.
- During bad times hurry up to a solution. Face your problems as soon as possible, good times will come soon.
- Full stomach, happy heart.
- It's not enough to lay an egg. You have to crow about it.
- Man proposes. God disposes. And the devil undoes it.
- No flies enter a closed mouth.
- No matter how early you get up, you can't make the sun rise any sooner.
- Poor musicians blame their instruments.
- The devil knows more because he is old rather than because he is a devil.
- The fishing's good in stormy waters.
- The shrimp that falls asleep is swept away by the current. You snooze, you lose.
- There is no competition among lighthouses.
- To want to is to be able to.
- We are as small as our joy and as big as our pain.
- Who disturbs the least helps a lot.
- Who does not live to serve does not serve to live.

- You don't check the teeth of a gifted horse. Be thankful for the gift, don't look for defects.

Mongolia

- A donkey that carries me is worth more than a horse that kicks me.
- A tiger wearing a bell will starve.
- Do not start if afraid, once begun do not be afraid.
- Don't look for bad things in the good that you do.
- Don't undo your bootlaces until you have seen the river.
- Each country's customs are different, just as each meadow's grass is different.
- Even foul water will quench fire.
- He who wants to build high must dig deep.
- If you are going to steal bells plug your ears.
- If you are sick, think about your life; if you are better, think about your gold.
- In a good word there are three winters' warmth; in one malicious word there is pain for six frosty months.
- It is easier to catch an escaped horse than to take back an escaped word.
- It's difficult to take a wolf cub without bringing in the whole pack.
- Men and women sleep on the same pillow, but they have different dreams.
- Once you have locked your door you are the emperor in your own domain.
- One idiot can ask more questions than ten wise men can answer.

- Rich is he who has no debts, fortunate he who lives without handicap.
- The distance between heaven and earth is no greater than one thought.
- The fish sees the bait not the hook; a man sees not the danger—only the profit.
- The meat-biting tooth is in the mouth; the man-biting tooth is in the soul.
- The more you listen the more you give yourself room for doubt.
- The supreme treasure is knowledge, the middle treasure is children, and the lowest treasure is material wealth.
- The winner has many friends, the loser has good friends.
- Times are not always the same; the grass is not always green.
- While horse is strong travel to see places.
- Wise men talk about ideas, intellectuals about facts, and the ordinary man talks about what he eats.
- You can't put two saddles on the same horse.

Montenegro

- Even his own tail is a burden to the weary fox.
- Every time the sheep bleats, she loses a mouthful.
- If you are going to visit the wolf take your dogs with you.
- Long hair, short wits, a woman's head.
- Marry with your ears and not with your eyes.
- When a fence is falling, every passer-by kicks it.
- Winter either bites with its teeth or lashes with its tail.
- Winter finds out what summer lays up.

Morocco

- A narrow space looks wide to the narrow-minded.
- A wise woman has much to say and yet remains silent.
- Better a patient man than a warrior, one who controls his temper than one who takes a city.
- For the sake of a single rose, the gardener becomes the servant to a thousand thorns.
- Little and lasting is better than much and passing.
- Love truth even if it harms you, and hate lies even if they serve you.
- The heart of a fool is in his mouth, the mouth of a wise man is in his heart.
- The mind is free, and the slightest thought has great influence. It is, therefore, important that you think enlightened thoughts.
- Though each path is different, there is only one way.

Mozambique

- A snake that you can see does not bite.
- He who led me in the night, will be thanked by me at daybreak.
- If you do not travel, you will marry your own sister.
- Never marry a woman who has bigger feet than you.
- No tattoo is made without blood.
- On a dead tree there are no monkeys.
- Once a man has been bitten by a lion, he buys a dog.
- Slander by the stream will be heard by the frogs.
- Witch doctors do not sell their potions to each other.
- You cannot dance well on only one leg.

Myanmar

- A genuine ruby wont sink and disappear in mud.
- A good character is real beauty that never fades.
- A ship-load of fish gets spoiled, because of one spoiled fish.
- Alertness and courage are life's shield.
- An unmarried woman is not honored, even if she has ten brothers.
- Beware of a man's shadow and a bee's sting.
- Collect the water while it rains.
- Do use a needle in time, or you might need an axe later.
- Don't use up your arrows before you go to battle.
- Even if the truth is buried for centuries, it will eventually come out and thrive.
- Excessive talk is sure to include errors.
- If there are too many teachers or leaders with different ideas, the follower will not do nothing and learn nothing.
- If you take big paces you leave big spaces.
- Many people count other people's faults and ignore their own.
- No child was ever born without having been conceived.
- No matter how much care is taken, someone will always be misled.
- Old cows like young grass.
- One sesame seed won't make oil.
- Only your real friends will tell you when your face is dirty.
- The child who is given everything he asks for usually won't

succeed in life.
- The excessively kind-hearted person becomes a slave.
- Two may become enemies, when their ideas are the same.
- Water can wear away even the hardest rock.
- You can be a king, if you are brave.

Namibia

- A diamonds father is coal, yet it regards itself as upper-class.
- A mother is always a mother.
- An old monkey never forgets how to climb trees.
- Envy and greed grow on the same stalk.
- From little date seeds, great things are born.
- Gold like the sun melts wax and hardens clay.
- It is the one who lies by a fire who feels the heat.
- Learning expands great souls.
- Let the first urge pass, wait for the second.
- Love is a despot who spares no one.
- Moral people sleep well at night, but the immoral seem to get pleasure from the waking hours much more.
- Only the mountains never meet.
- The earth is not ours, it is a treasure we hold in trust for future generations.
- The ways of the immoral are always predictable.
- Today butterflies, tomorrow wasps.
- When a tiny toe is hurting the whole-body stoops down to attend to it.
- When the fish gets rotten, it all starts from the head.

Nepal

- A speaker needs no tools.
- Depend on others and you'll go hungry.
- Even the devil slaves for the fortunate.
- Hold short services for minor gods.
- If you only depend on others, you will soon go hungry.
- It is the mind that wins or loses.
- Opportunities come but do not linger.
- The farmer grows the corn, but the bear eats it.
- The god who made the mouth will provide the food.
- To take revenge on an enemy, give him an elephant. First he must thank you for the gift, and then the elephant's appetite will deplete your enemy's resources.
- Too much sugar is bitter.
- Vanity blossoms but bears no fruit.
- Wealth is both an enemy and a friend.
- You have a lot of friends if you have money; otherwise there are only strangers.

Netherlands

- He who has spilt his porridge cannot scrape it all up again.
- Horse droppings are not figs.
- If the blind lead the blind, both will fall in the ditch.
- It depends on the fall of the cards.
- It is ill to swim against the current.
- One shears sheep, the other shears pigs.
- The whole world is upside down.
- They both crap through the same hole.
- Two dogs over one bone seldom agree.

New Zealand

- A house full of people is filled with different points of view.
- A little axe, when well used, brings lots of food.
- Don't spend time with people who don't respect you.
- Persist as tenaciously as you persist in eating.
- Survival is the treasured goal.
- There is more than one way to achieve a goal.
- Walk in the valley of our ancestors, learn of the history, and marvel at the beauty.

Nicaragua

- A favor given to man is appreciated by none.
- Envy follows merit like the shadow follows the body.
- Eyes that see do not grow old.
- Fleeing and running are not the same thing.
- It takes two to make a quarrel but only one to end it.
- Many things are too bad to be blessed, and too good to be cursed.
- Pretend you're in great danger, and you'll find out if you have any friends.
- Renounce a friend who covers you with his wings and destroys you with his beak.
- The lance never blunted the pen, nor the pen the lance.
- There is taste in variety, and variety in taste.
- There's nobody can prevent you getting into heaven, but there are many always ready to give you a shove into hell.
- There's nothing worse for an intelligent person than to put a fool beside him.

Niger

- A proverb is the horse of conversation: when the conversation lags, a proverb revives it.
- A wise man who knows proverbs can reconcile difficulties.
- Before one cooks, one must have the meat.
- If you watch your pot, your food will not burn.

Nigeria

- A forewarned battle will not kill a clever cripple.
- Give and take is what makes the life easy, a farmer that want to eat bread would send yam to the baker.
- If the lion wants to barb its mane it is not a dog that will be the barber.
- It is not hunger that makes a cat to be smaller than a tiger: It is its nature.
- It is the short name of theft they call pilfering.
- It is where the adult is that the child will grow to meet him.
- No matter how fast the horse gallops it will always meet the ground ahead.
- No one says a child should not be leprous if only he/she can stay alone in the forest.
- Nothing you can do to a pig to remove the protrusion of its mouth.
- One shouldn't put fire on one's roof top and sleep.
- Proverbs are the horses of words and words are that of proverbs: when words are lost, it is proverbs that we use to find them.
- The animal that is careful lives long in the forest.
- The cockerel shows being an elder by keeping the time but spoils it by defecating in the pen.
- The corpses weep for corpses and the mourners mourn themselves.
- The crouching of a tiger is not out of cowardice, it is only

looking for what to eat.

- The crowing of the cockerel brings misery to the sluggard.
- The fire covers itself with ashes on burnt out; the plantain replaces itself with suckers: it is children that will replace us when we die.
- The food that is given to a slave is not for body building but for survival.
- The lizard that enters into a scorpion's hole will come back with its rear.
- The man that had swam in the ocean and seas should not be afraid of a mere bathtub.
- The sky is wide enough for the birds to fly without collision.
- The stubbornness of the pepper seeds is not a thing of bother to the mill stone.
- Too much description turns a tiger to a mere deer.
- Twenty children cannot play together for twenty years.
- What you leave is what you meet: he who defecated on the road on his way to farm would meet flies when returning.
- When one buys clothe for the lazy man, one should also dye it.
- When you give a ram to the deity, you should let go of the rope.

Norway

- A hero is one who knows how to hang on one minute longer.
- Bad is called good when worse happens.
- Behind the clouds the sky is always blue.
- In every woman there is a queen. Speak to the queen and the queen will answer.
- Only book makes nobody wise.
- That which is loved is always beautiful.
- The more cooks, the more mess.
- The one who agrees with everyone agrees with no one.
- The one who wants to join the game, must taste the steak.
- There is no bad weather, only bad clothing.
- Those who want to sing will always find a song.
- You may go where you want, but you cannot escape yourself.

Oman

- Birds align with grain, but not with the stick.
- Build with silver and cover with gold.
- Do not leave todays homework for tomorrow.
- Every village has certain drawbacks to it.
- If your motive is good, a farting donkey won't harm you.
- Live near water and ask not about sustenance.
- The look is is a look, but the meaning is weak.
- What is late is great.
- Who has a habit, will never leave it even if his finger gets cut.

Pakistan

- A rich house makes its foolish inhabitants wise.
- Be yourself beautiful, and you will find the world full of beauty.
- Don't look down on anyone unless you are helping them up.
- If you do not marry a gentle woman, she will not bear you a gentle son.
- Look at a man's deeds, not whether he is tall or short.
- One who is free to sin, sins less; the very power weakens the seeds of sin.
- People who fight fire with fire usually end up with ashes.
- Pride is concerned with who is right. Humility is concerned with what is right.
- You can dress a monkey in a suit, but it is still a monkey.

Panama

- A proverb is to speech what salt is to food.
- Among the weak, the strongest is the one who doesn't forget his weakness.
- Half of an orange tastes just as sweet as a whole one.
- If there was not bad taste, goods would not be sold.
- If you want no disappointments, don't indulge in illusions.
- Speak whenever you must, hush whenever you can.
- The leafiest tree doesn't always have the juiciest fruit.
- The wise man affirms little and doubts much.
- Though you possess prudence, old man, do not despise advice.
- When the eyes see nothing, the heart feels nothing.
- Whether the pitcher strike the stone or the stone the pitcher, the pitcher suffers.

Paraguay

- A hatchet in the mouth is more harmful than a hatchet in the hand.
- Gratitude is the least of virtues; ingratitude is the worst of vices.
- It is a rarity to find someone who can weigh other people's faults without putting his own thumbs on the scale.
- Rare is the person who can weigh the faults of another without putting his thumb on the scale.

Peru

- Envy for a friend is like the taste of a sour pumpkin.
- Favor your own first, then others.
- Fortune and olives are alike: sometimes a man has an abundance and other times not any.
- From the tree of silence hands, the fruit of tranquility.
- Gold, when beaten, shines.
- If I listen, I have the advantage, if i speak others have it.
- It is better to prevent than to cure.
- Lawyer for the rich, scourge of the poor.
- Love looks through spectacles that make copper look like gold, poverty like riches, and tears like pearls.
- Only he who carries it knows how much the cross weighs.
- The child weeps for it's good and the old man for his ill.
- When the road is long, even slippers feel tight.
- Youth is intoxication without wine; old age, wine without intoxication.

Philippines

- A broom is sturdy because its strands are tightly bound.
- A clear conscience is far more valuable than money.
- A country without freedom is like a prisoner with shackled hands.
- A person who is outwardly calm has anger raging inside.
- A young branch can be straightened, a mature one breaks.
- Alertness and courage are life's shield.
- Children who get everything they ask for seldom succeed in life.
- He who does not know to look where he came from will never get to his destination.
- He who quits does not win, he who wins does not quit.
- It is easier to dam a river than to stop the flow of gossip.
- Laziness is the sibling of starvation.
- Life is like a wheel, sometimes at the top, sometimes at the bottom.
- Loyalty is more valuable than diamonds.
- One who spends too much time choosing ends up with cracked wares.
- People who do not break things first will never learn to create anything.
- The bitterness of studying is preferable to the bitterness of ignorance.
- The earth has ears, news has wings.
- The fly on the back of a water buffalo thinks that it's taller

than the buffalo.

- The person who is always criticizing others is usually the one who deserves criticism the most.
- There's no glory without sacrifice.
- Whatever the tree, so is the fruit.

Poland

- A flower without a smell is like a man without a soul.
- A pretty person looks pretty in everything.
- A success has many fathers, a failure is an orphan.
- Don't praise the day before sunset.
- Everyone judges according to themselves.
- Everywhere is fine, but the best at home.
- Hand washes hand, leg supports leg.
- Happiness is between the lips and the rim of a glass.
- How they see you, that's how they perceive you.
- If the goat didn't jump, she wouldn't have broken her leg.
- It's better to have a sparrow in your hand than a pigeon on the roof.
- Necessity is the mother of invention.
- The violin doesn't play for everybody.
- Those who argue, like each other.
- What one thinks when sober, one says when drunk.
- When the woman gets off the wagon, horses have an easier time.
- You become whom you befriend.

Portugal

- A good woman should be plump as a hen, with eyes dark as the midnight sky, and a disposition as fiery as pepper.
- A pot that over boils attracts the cook.
- An empty purse and a new house make a man wise, but too late.
- Better a big belly than starvation.
- Change yourself, and fortune will change.
- Dance in the streets you will learn to play music.
- Every peddler praises his own junk.
- Fish by fish the net becomes full.
- Good management is better than good income.
- Hell is paved with good intentions, roofed in with lost opportunities.
- If you live in a mud house, beware of storms.
- It is the one who sticks his hand in the stew pot who can feel how hot it is.
- Only a bull knows best its own desires and can best supply them.
- The hawk does not nest with the sparrow.
- The toad does not come into the daylight without reason.
- There is a remedy for everything; it is called death.
- Where you find a pig there is also slop.

Qatar

- A promise is an era.
- All who are running on their father's footsteps, are running
- Two captains sunk the ship.
- Who doesn't know the falcon will cook it.
- Who rides a donkey must be patient from the donkey's smell.

Romania

- A bad workman quarrels with his tools.
- A sin which is confessed is half forgiven.
- After the storm comes the good weather.
- Do not put your spoon into the pot which does not boil for you.
- Don`t give the sparrow in your hand for the crow on the fence.
- Don't put off for tomorrow whatever you can do today.
- If you wish good advice, consult an old man.
- Self-praise doesn`t smell good.
- The chip doesn`t jump too far from the stump.
- The one that digs someone else`s grave certainly falls there.
- The one that wakes up early will go far.
- The small stub overturns the big carriage.
- The smart promises and the stupid believe it.
- The true friend is known whenever you are in need.
- Too much talking makes one poor.
- Under a ragged coat lies wisdom.
- What the heart thinks, the tongue speaks.

Russia

- A tomtit in your hand is better than a crane in the sky.
- Do not have hundred rubles, rather have hundred friends.
- From time to time, it does not happen.
- If you have physical power, you do not need intelligence.
- It is better to see once than to hear hundred times.
- The first pancake is always lumpy.
- The wolves are full and sheep intact.
- Without effort, you cannot even pull a fish out of the pond.
- You cannot throw a word out of a song.

Rwanda

- A man's heart is not a sack open to all.
- Every cackling hen was an egg at first.
- Hens keep quiet when the cock is around.
- If you are building a house and a nail breaks, do you stop building, or do you change the nail?
- If your mouth turns into a knife, it will cut off your lips.
- In a court of fowls, the cockroach never wins his case.
- In a fiddler's house, all are dancers.
- When in someone else's home leave your defects at the door.
- When the child falls the mother weeps; when the mother falls the child laughs.
- When the leopard is away, his cubs are eaten.
- You can outdistance that which is running after you, but not what is running inside you.

Samoa

- A decision made at night may be changed in the morning.
- Blessed is the moon; it goes but it comes back again.
- Gather the breadfruit from the farthest branches first.
- Let each do his share of the work.
- Let the crab take counsel with its leg.
- Like a fish, one should look for a hole in the net.
- Only the snake looks at its slayer.
- The fault was committed in the bush, but it is now talked about on the highway.
- The grasshopper flies about, but the kingfisher watches him.
- The knee feels the tapping.
- The person who has burned their fingers often asks for tongs.

Scotland

- A plump widow needs no advertisement.
- Fools make feasts, and wise men eat them.
- Learn young, learn fair; learn old, learn more.
- Pierce the nagger's tongue with a thistle and you will hear no more complaints.
- Twelve highlanders and a bagpipe make a rebellion.
- What may be done at any time will be done at no time.
- When one is hungry, everything tastes good.

Senegal

- Haste and hurry can only bear children with many regrets along the way.
- If a centipede loses a leg, it does not prevent him from walking.
- If the eyes do not admire, the heart will not desire.
- It is better to be loved than feared.
- Lies that build are better than truths that destroy.
- People are man's medicine.
- The chameleon changes color to match the earth, the earth doesn't change color to match the chameleon.
- The frog likes water, but not boiling water.
- When a musician hath forgotten his note, He makes as though a crumb stuck in his throat.

Serbia

- A beaten man accepts what he is given.
- A dirty shoe still fits in a clean boot.
- A portly woman is always the best cook.
- A thorn pierces young skin more quickly than old.
- Build the barn before you buy the cow.
- Do not swat a mosquito with a sword.
- He who is on fire is not troubled by the smoke.
- There's no quiet child nor young grandmother.
- To know the path ahead, ask those returning.
- Trust but verify.
- Who has wine for dinner, he has water for breakfast.

Seychelles

- A well-fed old lion is better than a hungry young one.
- He who looks for honey must have the courage to face the bees.
- If a little tree grows in the shade of a larger tree, it will die small.
- The monkey leaps only as far as it can reach.
- When an elephant is in trouble even a frog will kick him.

Sierra Leone

- A black cow also gives white milk.
- A hundred aunts are not the same as one mother.
- A paddle here, a paddle there; the canoe stays still.
- An orange never bears a lime.
- Do not tell the man who is carrying you that he stinks.
- Even though chickens don't wash, their eggs are still white.
- He who refuses a gift will not fill his barn.
- He who upsets something should know how to put it back again.
- If you climb up a tree, you must climb down the same tree.
- Invite people into your parlor, and they will come into your bedroom.
- It is the wandering dog that finds the old bone.
- Knowledge is not the main thing, but deeds.
- Knowledge without practice makes but half an artist.
- Only a monkey understands a monkey.
- Proverbs are the children of experience.
- Quarrels end, but words once spoken never die.
- The big fish is caught with big bait.
- The cow must graze where she is tied.
- To try and fail is not laziness.
- When a single hair has fallen from your head, you are not yet bald.

Singapore

- A given excuse that was not asked for implies guilt.
- Better poverty before wealth than poverty after wealth.
- If you plant grass, you won't get rice.
- Not all stones are blessed to become diamonds.
- On a big tree, there are dead branches; in a big clan, there are beggars.
- Smart people put forth their mouth, dumb people put forth their hand.
- Those who speak aloud are boastful. Those who speak softly are unsure. Those who don't speak are dangerous.
- You don't need to teach a young crocodile to swim.

Slovakia

- Anger is an evil counselor.
- Better to eat bread in peace than cake amidst turmoil.
- Birds of the same feather flock together.
- Evil herb never dies out.
- One is apt to fall into the hole which he digs for another.
- Patience and time overcome all things.
- Slow but sure wins the race.
- What eyes don't see, heart doesn't hurt.
- Without caution even, cleverness is futile.

Slovenia

- A doorstep is the highest of all mountains.
- It is easier to believe than to go and ask.
- Man's life is like a drop of dew on a leaf.
- Never whisper to the deaf, or wink at the blind.
- Speak the truth but leave immediately after.
- What you build easily will fall quickly.

Solomon Islands

- An iron sharpens iron, so a pal sharpens a buddy.
- Your personal soul is nourished when you are type it is destroyed when you are cruel.

Somalia

- A camel can tolerate a heavy load, but not a crooked rope.
- A man with a sense of humor is never at a loss for words or action.
- A sinking person grabs a straw.
- Either be a mountain or lean on one.
- Even the brave is scared by a lion three times: first by its tracks, again by its roar, and one last time face to face.
- If people come together, they can even mend a crack in the sky.
- Ignorance is blindness.
- In the ocean, one does not need to sow water.
- Lend a false ear to false words.
- Only water in your hands can satisfy your thirst.
- Poverty is slavery.
- Sorrow is like rice in the store; if a basketful is removed every day, it will come to an end at last.
- The teeth and the tongue are close neighbors, and yet they sometimes bite each other.
- When the snake is in the house, one need not discuss the matter at length.

South Africa

- Almost doesn't fill a bowl.
- Even immortals are not immune to fate.
- Even the most beautiful flower withers in time.
- Guessing breeds suspicion.
- The lion is a beautiful animal when seen at a distance.
- The sun never sets that there has not been fresh news.
- When you bite indiscriminately, you end up eating your own tail.
- You can learn wisdom at your grandfather's feet, or at the end of a stick.
- You cannot know the good within yourself if you cannot see it in others.

Spain

- Acts are love and good reasons aren't.
- Don't leave the old road for a new trail.
- He/she erases with the elbow what his/her hand is doing.
- How nice it is to see the rain and not get wet.
- It isn't necessary to drown oneself in a glass of water.
- It never is late for learning.
- Love can do it all.
- Love is like water that never evaporates.
- Money does not last for fools.
- Something is something; less is nothing.
- The goat always heads toward the mountain.
- The shrimp that falls asleep is carried by the current.
- The tongue doesn't have a bone, but it cuts the thickest thing.
- There is not a worse deaf person than the one who doesn't want to hear.
- To govern is to foresee.
- To the best scribe comes a smudge.
- We all have a little bit of musician, poet and crazy person in ourselves.
- Where there's smoke, there's heat.

Sri Lanka

- Don't believe everything you hear, and don't tell everything you believe.
- During the daylight, a person will not fall into a pit that he fell into during the nighttime.
- If you can't do the deed, don't block another from trying.
- Make thyself a noble man before advising others.
- One cannot drink porridge without getting some on his moustache.
- The fool carries the burden.
- Think before you leap.
- When the dogs bark at the moon, the moon is not brought down because of it.

Sudan

- A dog cannot carry its puppies on its back.
- A little shrub may grow into a tree.
- A termite can do nothing to a stone save lick it.
- A young crocodile does not cry when he falls in the water.
- Don't cough in a hiding place.
- Ebb does not follow ebb; flood is in between.
- Even the sharpest ear cannot hear an ant singing.
- If you are wearing shoes, you don't fear the thorns.
- It is sad when the elephant dies, but the whole tribe can feed on it.
- The hand suffers at work, but the mouth still must eat.
- The poor are excused from washing with soap.
- When the monkey can't reach the ripe banana with his hand, he says it is not sweet.

Suriname

- If a person shaves you with a razor, do not shave him with broken glass.
- Salt doesn't boast it is salted.

Swaziland

- A man shows his character by what he laughs at.
- A man who prides himself on his ancestry is like the potato plant, the best part of which is underground.
- A person who says it cannot be done should not interrupt the man doing it.
- A traveler to distant places should make no enemies.
- The antelope that is constantly moving will fall in a pit.
- The bee that is forced into the hive will not produce honey.

Sweden

- A bashful dog rarely gets fat.
- A life without love is like a year without summer.
- Advice should be viewed from behind.
- Being young is a fault which improves daily.
- Friendship doubles our joy and divides our grief.
- In calm water every ship has a good captain.
- In spring no one thinks of the snow that fell last year.
- Love me when I least deserve it, because that's when I really need it.
- Luck never gives; it only lends.
- Noble deeds are done in silence.
- One should choose one's bedfellow whilst it is daylight.
- One should go invited to a friend in good fortune, and uninvited in misfortune.
- Shared joy is double joy. Shared sorrow is half sorrow.
- Sweep first before your own door before you sweep the doorsteps of your neighbors.
- The afternoon knows what the morning never suspected.
- The best place to find a helping hand is at the end of your arm.
- The butterfly often forgets it was a caterpillar.
- The cure for anything is salt water-sweat, tears, or the sea.
- Those who wish to sing always find a song.
- When a blind man carries a lame man, both go forward.
- When the cat's away, the rats dance on the table.

- Worry gives a small thing a big shadow.
- You cannot prevent the birds of sadness from passing over your head, but you can prevent them from nesting in your hair.

Switzerland

- A good spectator also creates.
- A greedy person and a pauper are practically one and the same.
- Ask ten brewers and you will get eleven opinions.
- At the bottom of the sack you will find the bill.
- Better to sell with regret than to keep with regret.
- Great consolation may grow out of the smallest saying.
- He who mocks the cripple should be straight himself.
- In a house of gold, the clocks are of lead.
- It is easier to criticize than to do better.
- One simple maxim is often worth more than two good friends.
- Sometimes you have to be silent in order to be heard.
- The night rinses what the day has soaped.
- The poor lack much, but the greedy lack more.
- The tongue is the worst piece of meat in the world.
- To be a fool at the right time is also an art.
- When in doubt who will win, be neutral.
- Who cares about every little feather should not make the bed.
- Words are dwarfs, deeds are giants.

Syria

- Even paradise is no fun without people.
- He who has his hand in the water is not like him who has his hand in the fire.
- It is an easy thing to find a staff to beat a dog.
- It's better to deal with the devil we know than the devil we don't know.
- The cloth of shame does not warm and if it does, it does so only briefly.
- The land is cultivated by its own oxen.
- Writing is the mother of eloquence and the father of artists.

Tahiti

- Every man is the builder of his own hut.
- Goods given make quicker return than goods held.
- If you aim your spear at two fish, both will escape.
- Ignorance doesn't kill you, but it will make you sweat a lot.
- It is never too late to give to those who do not have.
- Never fear the sea, fear the storm.
- The coral waxes, the palm grows, but man departs.
- The life of the land is the life of the people.
- The older a man gets, the larger the waves become.
- The well-trodden path is not always the right path.
- When the shark laughs with the dolphin, there is a devilish spirit at play.

Taiwan

- A husband and wife often fight intensely at one moment and then kiss intensely at the next moment.
- Even champions make mistakes. There is no one who doesn't.
- Greed will cause pain.
- If someone transports dung and does not eat it, it should not be concluded that he is an honest person.
- It takes sweat to work on things, but it only takes saliva to criticize things.
- Many students have become kings or queens, but no teachers have.
- Something that looks good does not necessarily taste good.

Tanzania

- A sheep cannot bleat in two different places at the same time.
- Do not mend your neighbor's fence before seeing to your own.
- Even flies have ears.
- Everything has an end.
- In the world all things are two and two.
- Little by little, a little becomes a lot.
- One who bathes willingly with cold water doesn't feel the cold.
- We start as fools and become wise through experience.

Thailand

- Bad seven times, good seven times.
- Catch a fish with two hands.
- When the cat is not there, the mice are happy.
- When the water rises, hurry to get some
- You have to lose something to get another thing.

Tibet

- A child without education is like a bird without wings.
- A person suffering from jaundice sees a white conch-shell as yellow.
- A wise man's quick thought is not apart from knowledge.
- Although garlic may be eaten in secrecy, its smell can be sniffed from afar.
- Ask others for opinions but decide on your own.
- Better than the young man's knowledge is the old man's experience.
- Cure the illness that is not yet an illness.
- Discipline must be endured by oneself before one set other under it.
- Don't trust a hungry man to watch your rice.
- Even poison can be turned to medicine if one is versed in the art of healing.
- Frank words make listening easier.
- Honor a king in his own land; honor a wise man everywhere.
- If the soldiers are cowards, it does not matter how big the army is.
- In times of hardship don't play truant.
- Knowing just one word of wisdom is like knowing a hundred ordinary words
- Let go of your dignity within your own family, maintain your dignity in the face of other tribes.
- One sort of art is the art of living an ordinary life in an

extraordinary manner.

- Pleasant conversation may be of some help also during times of sorrow.
- The blacksmith thinks making butter is difficult; the buttermaker thinks casting iron is difficult.
- The parrot is put into a cage for its skill of speech; the other birds enjoy the freedom of the sky.
- The wise man's wealth lies in good deeds.
- The wise understand; fools follow the reports of others.
- Violently abused, even a kind, friendly person becomes an enemy.
- Watch your character; it becomes your destiny.
- When the circumstances are not examined before one speaks, even a clever man may be no better than a blundering fool.
- Who gets stuck in trivial prosperity will not attain great prosperity.

Togo

- A woman's tongue is sharp enough to pierce the toughest flesh.
- Absence polishes passion, presence reinforces it.
- Breed up a serpent and he will strike when you are in deep slumber.
- Every rhinoceros is proud of its horn.
- Good stew is best to be made in an old pot.
- If there is no traitor in your house, the witches will never be able to get at you.
- If you hurt the reputation of another, you damage your own.
- In the world there is more madness than sanity.
- It is impossible to go and look into the stomach of another.
- Not all those who are old are wise.
- The heart rules without rules.
- The man who has never experienced evil does not know the worth of what is good.
- The tears running down your face do not blind you.

Trinidad and Tobago

- Children turn out like their parents.
- Everyone finds their place in life.
- Not all useful knowledge comes from books or formal learning.
- People never recognize their own faults.
- The race is not for the swift, slow and steady wins.
- The thing that makes you happy may also hurt you.
- The young and inexperienced don't understand true troubles or hardships.

Tunisia

- He who is covered with other people's clothes is naked.
- How lovely is the sun after rain, and how lovely is laughter after sorrow?
- If someone hits you with a stone, hit him with bread; your bread will return to you and his stone will return to him.
- No one will say, "My father is incontinent.". Everyone will say, "He is a man of advice and wisdom.".
- The multitude is stronger than the king.
- Who came back from the grave and told the story?

Turkey

- A defeated wrestler never tires of wrestling again.
- A man is as wise as his head, not his age.
- A tribulation is better than a hundred warnings.
- An ember burns where it falls.
- An over-protected eye gets the speck.
- Beauty passes, wisdom remains.
- Do not search for a calf under a bull.
- Heart endures when eye does not see.
- If one is far away, one also gets far away from the heart.
- It is not disgraceful to ask, it is disgraceful no to know.
- It takes two hands to make a sound.
- Kind words will get a snake out of its hole.
- Many will point to the right way after the wheel is broken.
- One who does not slap his children, will slap his knees.
- One who handles honey, licks his fingers.
- One who sows wind will reap hurricane.
- Strong vinegar only damages its container.
- The one who asks has one side of his face dark; the one who refuses to give has both sides.
- The rich man's wealth tires the poor man's jaw.
- The sheep separated from the flock gets eaten by the wolf.
- The tree branch should be bent when it is young.
- To the raven's eye, its chickens look like falcons.
- What a man is at seven is also what he is at seventy.
- You can't run a water mill by carrying water.

Uganda

- A dog with a bone in his mouth cannot bite you.
- An elephant can never fail to carry its tusks.
- Caution is not cowardice; even the ants march armed.
- Do not belittle what you did not cultivate.
- Empty hands only please their owner.
- Even the mightiest eagle comes down to the treetops to rest.
- He who loves, loves you with your dirt.
- In the home of the coward they laugh while in the home of the brave they cry.
- It is better that trials come to you in the beginning and you find peace afterwards than that they come to you at the end.
- Old men sit in the shade because they planted a tree many years before.
- Polygamy makes a husband a double-tongued man.
- The bird that pecks at a rock trusts in the strength of its beak.

Ukraine

- Act swiftly, think slowly.
- Live one century, study one century.
- Love tells us many things that are not so.
- Luck always seems to be against the man who depends on it.
- No man deserves punishment for his thoughts.
- No matter how hard you try, a bull will never give milk.
- The fatter the flea the leaner the dog.
- The mother remembers her youth and so does not trust her daughter.
- To him that you tell your secret you resign your liberty.
- When the banner is unfurled, all reason is in the trumpet.
- With patience, it is possible to dig a well with a teaspoon.

United Kingdom

- A stitch in time saves nine.
- Bad news travels fast.
- Better untaught than ill taught.
- Birds of a feather flock together.
- Don't cross your bridges before you come to them.
- Don't look a gift horse in the mouth.
- Every cloud has a silver lining.
- It was the last straw that broke the camel's back.
- Live and let live.
- Marry in haste and repent at leisure.
- Nothing ventured nothing gained.
- One man's meat is another man's poison.
- Out of the frying pan into the fire.
- Soon learnt, soon forgotten.
- The best advice is found on the pillow
- The best things in life are free.
- The grass is always greener on the other side.
- The way to a man's heart is through his stomach.
- Where there is a will there is a way.
- You can lead a horse to water, but you cannot make it drink.
- You can't judge a book by its cover.

Uruguay

- Better to lose a minute in your life than your life in a minute.
- Better to marry a neighbor than a stranger.
- Gifts break rocks and melt hearts.
- That which is done at night appears in the day.
- Time will give you the best disguise.

USA

- Absence makes the heart grow fonder.
- Actions speaks louder than words.
- All is fair in love and war.
- Beggars can't be choosers.
- Better late than never.
- Early to bed, early to rise makes a man healthy, wealthy, and wise.
- Easy come, easy go.
- Give someone an inch, he/she will take a mile.
- Honesty is the best policy.
- Let bygones be bygones.
- Nothing ventured, nothing gained.
- Seeing is believing.
- There are plenty of other fishes in the sea.

Uzbekistan

- A word said is a shot fired.
- Don't choose a house; choose neighbors. Don't choose a path; choose traveling companions.
- Have breakfast yourself; share lunch with your friend; and give dinner to your enemy.
- He who possesses knowledge possesses the world.

Venezuela

- A good friend will fit you like ring to finger.
- He who doesn't look ahead gets left behind.
- Join with good men and you will be one of them.
- One sword keeps another in its scabbard.
- Proverbs in conversation are torches in darkness.
- Treat the lesser as you would have the greater treat you.
- When the hare leaps, there are no lame greyhounds.

Vietnam

- A swallow doesn't make a spring.
- When eating a fruit, think of the person who planted the tree.
- A day of travelling will bring a basket full of learning.
- Adversity is the mother of wisdom.
- One drop of poison infects the whole tun of wine.
- Never offer to teach fish to swim.
- A fair face may hide a foul heart.
- Fortune favors the brave.
- Haste makes waste.
- If you run after two hares, you'll catch neither.
- Constant dripping hollows out the stone.
- You can catch more flies with honey than with vinegar.
- The higher you climb, the more you hurt if you fall.

Wales

- A nation without a language is a nation without a heart.
- Better a good shilling than a dud sovereign.
- Better my own cottage than the palace of another.
- He who has no faults is not born.
- Let not your tongue cut your throat.
- Memory slips, letters remain.
- Speak well of your friend; of your enemy, say nothing.
- Starting the work is two thirds of it.
- Tapping persistently breaks the stone.
- The greater the hurry, the more obstacles there are.
- The old feel the blows suffered when young.

Yemen

- A foreigner should be well-behaved.
- Every sickness begins in the stomach.
- He who eats well can face an army.
- He who is patient is always successful.
- It is better to wear mended clothes than being without clothes or bare.
- Setting the conditions before you make an agreement is better than having an argument in the middle of the work.
- The master of the people is their servant.
- Whoever does not help himself cannot help others.

Zambia

- A child that does not travel praises his mother as the best cook.
- A cow does not find its own horns heavy.
- If you followed what a chicken eats, would you eat the chicken?
- Talk to a person who can understand and cook for a person who can be satisfied.
- The shark who has eaten cannot swim with the shark that is hungry.
- To get rid of anger, first weed out the bitter roots.
- Two thighs will always rub together
- You have to look after wealth, but knowledge looks after you.

Zimbabwe

- A coward has no scar.
- A ripened fruit does not cling to the vine.
- An elephant's tusks are never too heavy for it.
- Between true friends even water drunk together is sweet enough.
- Don't throw out the old pot until you have the tinker makes a new one.
- If words fail, no others will avail.
- If you can walk you can dance, if you can talk you can sing.
- Passion is of greater consequence than facts.
- People who do not mend things first will never produce something.
- Proverbs can be applied to get what you want.
- The monkey does not see his own hind backside; he sees his neighbor's.
- Two rats cannot share the same hole.
- Until the lion tells his side of the story, the tale of the hunt will always glorify the hunter.
- Whoever plows with a team of donkeys must have patience.
- You cannot tell a hungry child that you gave him food yesterday.

Don't miss out!

Visit the website below and you can sign up to receive emails whenever Emre Imer publishes a new book. There's no charge and no obligation.

https://books2read.com/r/B-A-KAEH-BDUV

BOOKS 2 READ

Connecting independent readers to independent writers.

Made in the USA
Monee, IL
07 June 2022

97612974R00114